Seventy Seven
Irrefutable Truths of Marriage

Seventy Seven
Irrefutable Truths of Marriage

Dr. LARRY & JUDI KEEFAUVER

Bridge-Logos *Publishers*

Gainesville, Florida 32614 USA

All Scriptures are from the *New King James Version* unless otherwise indicated.

Disclaimer:
Throughout this book, we have attempted to alternate the use of "he, him" and "she, her" in the chapters. Simply remember that if the pronoun refers to "him," the wife is not off the hook and vice versa. All these truths apply to both mates except for Truth # 65, which is directed to husbands specifically.

Seventy Seven Irrefutable Truths of Marriage
By Dr. Larry and Judi Keefauver
Copyright 2002
Library of Congress Catalog Number: Pending
International Standard Book Number 0-88270-908-9
Reprinted 2003

Published By:
Bridge-Logos
Gainesville, FL 32614

bridgelogos.com

CONTENTS

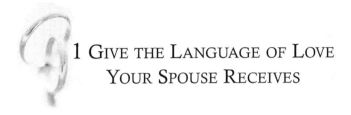

1 GIVE THE LANGUAGE OF LOVE YOUR SPOUSE RECEIVES

"Have you heard about the five languages of love?" the seminar participant asked. My memory was jogged. Of course, Gary Chapman's list immediately came to mind: gift giving, acts of service, words of affirmation, quality time and physical touch.

Each of us has an expressive and a receptive preference in these languages of love. For example, I may prefer to give gifts as my expressive love language. So I bring my wife all kinds of gifts to say to her, "I love you." But her receptive love language may be quality time. If I fail to spend enough quality time with her, all the gifts in the world will never adequately communicate to her my love and devotion.

Try this: Find out your mate's receptive love language. Express your love in all the love languages, but spend the most effort in giving to him what he needs instead of want you want to give.

Remember to love your mate with his receptive love language. Love seeks the best for your spouse.

Love suffers long and is kind; love does not envy;
love does not parade itself, is not puffed up;
does not behave rudely, does not seek its own,
is not provoked, thinks no evil;
does not rejoice in iniquity, but rejoices in the truth;
bears all things, believes all things, hopes all things,
endures all things. Love never fails.

1 Cor.13:4-8

1

2 RECHARGE
YOUR MATE'S EMOTIONAL BANK
WITH AFFIRMATION EACH MORNING

"**D**oesn't all that I did for you yesterday count for anything today?" asked the frustrated husband.

It's a new day. Have fresh love and affirmation for today. It's not that yesterday's expressions of love don't count. They have built a foundation for today's fresh expressions. But never rest on yesterday's laurels.

A new bouquet of flowers needs to replace the old, wilting one. My wife mentioned a vase of dried flowers sitting on the kitchen counter. "I really love those flowers, but they're months old. Will they ever be replaced?"

Yes, the memory of receiving those roses months ago was touching and wonderful. But memory doesn't meet today's need.

Be fresh and creative today. Find a new way to say, "I love you." The emotional bank needs refilling; without recognizing this, today's journey of love could easily run out of gas!

Today's neglect may quickly negate pleasant memories of past expressions of love. You and your spouse need fresh, new and exciting ways to express to each other today, "I love you."

Try this: Write "I love you!" on the bathroom mirror with a marker. Put a Scripture underneath it.

Therefore, if anyone is in Christ,
he is a new creation; old things have passed away.

2 Cor. 5:17

3 BE GRATEFUL

Everyone around the table stuffed their mouths with the tasty meal. But at the end, no one said, "Thanks."

The wife and mother had worked hard to prepare the evening meal for her family. I was a guest at the table. Everyone seemed to love one another. Everyone enjoyed the meal and appeared happy. But an attitude of gratitude was lacking.

Perhaps everyone simply expected a good meal to be prepared. Perhaps they now took for granted what was given to them out of love. But no matter how common, routine or expected love is, it's always a gift for which we give thanks.

Every mate loves to hear a thank-you, even if that expression of love has been repeated hundreds of time. Gratitude never gets old or wears out.

"But my spouse should know how I feel," protests the hurried mate. Knowing how one feels and hearing it expressed are two totally different things. "Out of the heart the mouth speaks." So if gratitude is in your heart, say it. And if it's not, pray that God changes you and gives you a heart of thanksgiving instead of a heart of expectation.

Try this: Sit down facing one another. Let the husband go first. For one minute, the husband thanks God out loud for all that he appreciates about his wife. Then the wife thanks God out loud for one minute for her husband. Do these one-minute thanksgiving prayers together often!

In everything give thanks; for this is the will of God in Christ Jesus for you.

1 Thess. 5:18

3

4 Be Kind to Your Mate

"What is the number one advice you would give to couples in marriage counseling?" I asked Dr. Wayne Oates, the renowned marriage counselor and prolific author.

Without a pause, the sage replied, "Be kind to one another." It sounded too simple. But reality is that kindness is the last thing on an angry couple's minds. Too often they want to hurt one another to repay the hurt they have received from their mate's words or acts of unkindness.

Kindness involves caring for the other person more than yourself. Kindness chooses to speak life instead of death. Kindness finds a way to forgive instead of blame. Kindness expresses affirmation instead of condemnation.

Kindness becomes very difficult when one has negative feelings toward a mate. But kindness helps defuse the pain and begins to rebuild and restore the love in a relationship.

What was the last kind thing you did to let your mate know that you esteemed her beyond yourself? How soon will you express kindness again?

Try this: Bring home some fresh flowers. It's a Jewish custom to celebrate the beginning of the Sabbath on Friday evenings with flowers on the dinner table. Make it a practice each Friday.

And be kind to one another, tenderhearted, forgiving one another, just as God in Christ forgave you.

Eph. 4:32

5 BELIEVE THE BEST ABOUT YOUR MATE

"What did you really mean when you did that?" asked the angry, suspicious wife. This particular wife always believed her husband was "up to no good."

First, let's admit that love is a gift and trust must be earned. This husband had violated his wife's trust on many occasions. However, he deeply loved his wife. The promises he broke were more irritating than devastating. But she chose to always believe the worst about him.

Second, let's remember that one reason both of you got married was out of love for one another. So what your spouse does or says has its roots in love, not in bad intentions.

Even when your spouse fails to keep a promise or fulfill an expectation, that spouse isn't a failure. The best way to believe the best about your mate is to remember his first love instead of his last mistake.

Believing the best about your spouse builds on hope instead of despair, and trust instead of doubt.

When we love one another with God's love, then we expect the best and are surprised if the worst ever happens. Set aside the past. Start expecting the best now!

Try this: Begin praying thanksgiving to God for all the fruit of the Spirit in your mate's heart: peace, love, joy, patience, goodness, kindness, faithfulness, humbleness and self-control.

[Love] always looks for the best, never looks back, but keeps going to the end.

1 Cor. 13, The Message

5

6 BLESS AND PROSPER
EACH OTHER

"**I** have never laid hands on and blessed my spouse," replied the perplexed husband. Why not bless your spouse as often as possible?

In the Old Testament, fathers often laid hands on their children and spoke a blessing. In the New Testament, early Christian leaders often laid hands on people to impart God's Spirit and blessing as those people served the church or went out to preach the gospel.

Why not bless your spouse? Pray a blessing for prosperity, health, wholeness and intimacy with God. Pray for God's Spirit to anoint your spouse with power, wisdom and favor at home and work.

Blessing speaks God's shalom over a person. Shalom means more than peace; it connotes well-being, wholeness, health and prosperity.

So take time today to bless your spouse. Pray for God's blessing to overflow in her life. Speak God's shalom into every thing she does and every relationship she has.

Try this: Lay hands on your spouse's head and pray Numbers 6, the Aaronic blessing, over your spouse. Let that blessing be the oil of gladness poured over your mate.

The LORD bless you and keep you;
the LORD make his face shine upon you
and be gracious to you;
the LORD turn his face toward you
and give you peace.

Num. 6:24-26 NIV

6

7 BUILD
ON EACH OTHER'S STRENGTHS

When you really know someone it's so easy to dwell on weakness instead of strength. The focus often becomes negative instead of positive. A husband or wife tries to correct and change instead of accept and pray.

One of the most common prayers in marriage is, "Lord, change my wife," or, "Lord, change my husband." The mature prayer of marriage is, "Lord, change me." Let the Lord change and correct your spouse. Spend your time praying and building on strengths.

At the beginning of marriage counseling, I often ask two questions:

What did you love about your mate when you first married?

What ten strengths do you appreciate about your mate right now?

That often seems to shock the couple. They are coming to a counselor to tell all the bad stuff. But reiterating the negative never heals; it only hurts.

Focus on the strengths in your marriage. Begin to release the weaknesses.

Try this: List all of your mate's strengths. Begin focusing on strengthening his strengths.

Fix your thoughts on what is true and good and right.
Think about things that are pure and lovely,
and dwell on the fine, good things in others.
Think about all you can praise God for
and be glad about.

Phil. 4:8 TLB

8 DON'T LET ONE BAD DAY RUIN A GOOD WEEK

"You just ruined my week," screamed the husband as he slammed the door and bolted toward his car and off to work.

That's hogwash! Nobody can ruin your day or your week unless you let them. Truthfully, one bad day doesn't undo all the good days. Think about it. In baseball, an all-star batter may only get a hit one out of three times at bat. Those two misses don't negate the hit. A .333 batting average is excellent.

Likewise, six great days of sharing, intimacy, growth and progress in marriage should never be negated by one bad day of setbacks or difficulties.

So what if you fail ever so often? So what if you or your spouse take a step back after three or four steps forward? All is not lost. It's only a hiccup, not a heart attack!

My wife, Judi, is a nurse. She often helps people through relational crises by putting things in perspective. She'll say, "Well, is it life or death? If it's not life-threatening, you'll survive."

Stop making every molehill into a mountain. Don't escalate a problem into a crisis. After all, life is problem-solving. Get used to valleys and stop expecting continuous mountaintops.

Try this: The next time you or your spouse makes a mistake, say, "Remember the last great thing you did? It was _____. It far outweighs this small problem. Let's forgive, forget and forge ahead."

If they fall it isn't fatal,
for the Lord holds them with his hand.

Ps. 37:24 TLB

9 DON'T COMPARE
YOUR MARRIAGE TO OTHERS;
COMPARE IT ONLY TO GOD'S TRUTH

"Well, I'm certainly a better husband than Joe," protested a defensive husband in counseling. Truthfully, we can always find someone else better or worse than ourselves. It's important to emphasize how far we've come, but the key to a successful marriage rests in not just starting strong and making progress. Success culminates in finishing strong.

We measure growth in marriage by our progress in becoming like Jesus and His love for His bride, the Church. What are some of the essential qualities of the relationship of Christ to His Church and the Bridegroom to the bride?

Unconditional love (agape)—His love desires the best for the other person. Marriage is not about me; it's about my mate. Love says, "Nothing can make me stop loving you."

Servant attitude and lifestyle—Submit to one another out of reverence for Christ (Eph. 5:21 NIV). Ask your mate, "How may I serve you?"

Sacrificial friendship—Friends lay down their lives for one another (John 15:13). Jesus laid down His life for the Church. Say to your spouse, " You're my best friend."

Honoring and esteeming your mate—Jesus presents His bride as a glorious, purified mate. We honor and esteem our mates, preferring them to ourselves.

Try this: How can you honor your spouse today? What can you do to honor your mate before others? Do it.

Let nothing be done through selfish ambition
or conceit, but in lowliness of mind let each
esteem others better than himself.

Phil. 2:4

9

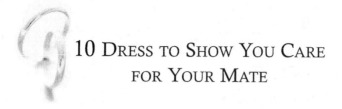

10 Dress to Show You Care for Your Mate

"How can you leave the house looking like that? I have to be seen with you!" commented the wife. Now the husband could respond childishly and say, "You're not my mother. Don't tell me how to dress."

Or that husband could respond maturely and change what he is wearing. Why? Because we dress for our mates. We look good for them. We want to dress sharply, attractively and modestly for them.

At times, we see couples walking through the mall and one of the pair is dressed so provocatively that everyone is looking at them, except the mate. We dress for our mates, not for others.

Consider this: your clothes, hairstyle, scent, weight and total appearance honors Christ and your mate. Of course God sees the heart, not the outer appearance. But the outer appearance reflects what's in the heart.

If you have a heart for your spouse, then you will dress to please both your spouse and Christ.

Try this: Go shopping with your mate. Try on and select clothing that you both enjoy and find attractive.

Remember that how you both dress sends a message about self-image and your marriage to the world around you. Before you go out, check out your appearance in the mirror of your mate's vision.

Ask, "Does this outfit please you and the Lord?"

...Make up your mind not to put any stumbling block or obstacle in your brother's way.

Rom. 14:13b

10

11 Enjoy Physical Intimacy

Sexual fulfillment and fun are part of the joy of marriage. It's not a duty; it's a privilege to share physical intimacy with one another. Discover what pleases and fulfills your mate. Talk about what brings your spouse pleasure and fulfillment. Then do it.

Make time for foreplay. Everything preceding physical intimacy is part of foreplay. Don't rush your time together. Put your mate's needs above your own. As you meet your spouse's needs, you will discover your own needs being met.

Remember that the goal of physical intimacy can be something other than intercourse. Touching, talking, hugging and time together produce powerful intimacy. Have fun. Relax. Focus on your mate's needs.

Stop thinking about other things, problems or people when you are being physically intimate with one another. Give your total attention to your mate. Find times for just the two of you to get away from children, jobs, responsibilities, etc. Spend one-on-one time together daily.

Try this: Decide how much one-on-one time you will spend together daily. Use that time to share positively and be physically intimate.

Do not deprive each other except by mutual consent and for a time, so that you may devote yourselves to prayer. Then come together again so that Satan will not tempt you because of your lack of self-control.

1 Cor. 7:5 NIV

12 Guard Your Tongue and Speak Life

"I'm so sorry, dear. I didn't mean to say that," the wife explained to her husband. Have you ever offered such a weak apology?

The truth is, we really do mean what we say. Jesus confirmed this, "For out of the overflow of the heart the mouth speaks" (Matt. 12:34b NIV). If it were not in our hearts, then we wouldn't say it.

Proverbs 18 reminds us that life and death are in the power of the tongue. Life is only speaking what the Father tells you to say to your spouse. Death is speaking out of your flesh—your hurt, anger and pain.

Speaking life is:

Affirming your mate's character and actions.

Accepting your mate's strengths.

Encouraging your mate's destiny and potential.

Listening before you speak.

Sharing the truth in love.

Repenting quickly.

Forgiving even before your mate repents.

Saying only what the Father tells you to say.

What can be done if your spouse is speaking death to you? Interrupt respectfully and ask, "Did the Father tell you to say that?" Try this. Ask your partner to pray before she proceeds. If your partner keeps speaking death, refuse to listen. Explain that you do not choose to receive death, and then leave the room.

Death and life are in the power of the tongue,
And those who love it will eat its fruit.

Prov. 18:20-21

13 KEEP PASSION ALIVE

"I am so tired of doing everything the same old way," moaned the distressed spouse. Insanity is doing the same thing the same way and expecting different results. God uses passion to produce breakthroughs in your marriage.

What is passion? It's an intense love and desire to grow together as one in Christ. At times love loses its initial fire, not because romance has left the marriage, but because we give too many other things the priority of our attention and focus.

While courting and preparing for marriage, a couple's primary focus is one another. That singular focus produces passion. But after the honeymoon, distractions begin to grow in the marriage like weeds. Such distractions cool down passion like removing logs from a fire.

Try this: Some practical steps you can take to keep the passion alive are:

Daily spend one-on-one time together.

Get away together regularly.

Identify distractions and minimize them. For example, turn off the phone during times you want to be together. Turn off the TV and spend time talking with one another.

Fill your weeks with unexpected surprises. Give gifts, make calls, have dates and have fun with one another.

For your love is better than wine.

Song 1:2

14 LAUGH WITH ONE ANOTHER

"I love to see couples laughing together," the waitress said to us. We had just recalled a funny time with our grandchildren and were laughing uncontrollably together.

Judi has a favorite saying, "Lighten up. It's not life or death." As a nurse, she dealt with terminal illness and critical situations daily. Some of the mundane stuff in life can drain the fun out of living and loving together.

Become accustomed to the fact that life is problem-solving. You can approach problems with a sense of humor and overcome the circumstances. Or you can live "under the circumstances" and make every problem a crisis.

Some marriages look like survival camps; every day is filled with heavy, weighty junk. But even persecuted peoples in history have developed "gallows humor" to overcome their plight.

Marriage isn't a life-sentence; it's a sentence to life. Enjoy the journey. Laugh at the circumstances and with each other. Have fun.

Let joy be your inner fuel for getting through your valleys together. Your spouse is a gift of joy to lift you up when you're down.

Try this: Get a silly joke book. Take time to read it to each other. Make a decision to laugh at your problems instead of crying over them. Remember that tears last only for a season, but joy is eternal.

Rejoice in the Lord always. Again I will say, rejoice!

Phil. 4:4-5

15 GIVE LOVE; EARN TRUST

The hurting, betrayed wife moaned, "I don't think I can ever trust him again." I realized then that love is a gift, but trust must be earned.

Believing the best about my spouse is a matter of trust, not love. No matter what he has said, I trust that person based on what he did. If he promised to be home at a certain time and failed to appear, then my trust erodes. If he promised to complete a task and the job was forgotten, then my trust becomes tentative the next time a promise is made.

But I want to trust. I desire to believe the best about my mate. I want to feel that, no matter what, their intentions are good and virtuous.

So what will I do? I will decide to trust again. Yes, renewed trust can be disappointed. But consider for a moment the alternative. If I question every motive, if I mistrust every promise, then I can never experience intimacy with my spouse.

Every act of trust risks hurt. But trusting love can overcome the fear of being hurt. Decide to believe the best. How? Begin with forgiveness. Ask for truthfulness. Proceed with faith. And decide that you can believe the best about another imperfect person who is much like yourself.

Try this: Ask for forgiveness even if you feel right and think that your spouse is wrong. Try saying this, "Will you forgive me for _____?"

There is no fear in love; but perfect love casts out fear, because fear involves torment.

1 John 4:18

16 LOVE UNCONDITIONALLY

"There is nothing you can do to make me stop loving you," read the plaque on the pastor's desk. "Yeah, right!" I thought. Instead of focusing on the conversation, I began to think of all the things I might do to upset him. Foolish thoughts, but they were real feelings.

No one can make us feel any way. Our feelings belong to us. We choose how we feel. So my mate can't make me angry or make me love him or her. Love has feeling, but it's more than a feeling—love is an act of will. I choose to love even when I don't feel loving or my mate is acting unlovely.

Unconditional love...seeks the best, prefers my spouse's needs over my own, cares deeply, listens attentively, makes a lifelong decision to forgive, speaks the truth in love, sacrifices immediate gratification for long-term relationship.

Try this: Find out the top needs your spouse has, such as security, affirmation, time with you, etc. Decide to meet those needs consistently with your best effort.

Love is patient, love is kind. It does not envy,
it does not boast, it is not proud. It is not rude,
it is not self-seeking, it is not easily angered,
it keeps no record of wrongs.

Love does not delight in evil but rejoices
with the truth. It always protects, always trusts,
always hopes, always perseveres. Love never fails.

1 Cor. 13:4-8 NIV

17 NEVER PUBLICLY EXPOSE OR RIDICULE YOUR MATE

My wife and I were having dinner with another couple when the husband told an embarrassing story about his wife. Everyone blushed but him. Another time, we were visiting a congregation and listening to the pastor tell story after story about his wife and children. His humor made his wife look silly and ridiculous.

Few things can rip a marriage apart with more devastation than public ridicule. Making fun of your spouse or demeaning him reveals your lack of esteem and honor. Take these steps to avoid exposing and demeaning your spouse in public:

Never tell jokes with your spouse as the punch line.

Get permission from your spouse to tell any personal stories.

Decide always to honor and praise your mate in public.

Make remarks about your mate that show how you cherish and care for him or her.

Refuse to listen to others who degrade their mates.

Refuse to tell off-color or ethnically disparaging jokes about anyone, including your mate.

Treat your mate in public the way you want to be treated.

Try this: Ask your spouse to tell you honestly what you do or say in public that embarrasses him. Then stop doing or saying that.

A wholesome tongue is a tree of life.   Prov. 15:4

18 NEVER TAKE YOUR MATE FOR GRANTED

"**M**y wife always cooks breakfast for me," boasted the husband.

"Do you thank her every time?" I asked.

"Of course not; that would be silly. She has always done it," he replied.

Whatever your mate does for you needs to be noticed with a smile, a grateful remark or a kind action in return. It's so easy to take one another for granted. But doing so reveals an ungrateful heart.

Jesus was an expert at taking notice of people. He particularly noticed those who served and ministered to Him. You can do the same.

Husbands should not take for granted clean toilets, ironed shirts, laundry, cooked meals, etc. Wives should not take for granted yard work, washed cars, trash taken out, etc.

Don't get this wrong. I'm not suggesting that there are typical things a husband or wife does. I'm only suggesting that whatever is done as an expression of love and service should never go unnoticed.

Try this: Begin noticing every expression of love your mate says or does.

Find creative ways to say thank you like writing with a marker on the mirror in the bathroom your expression of gratitude. Leave thank you notes in unusual places like luggage and laundry.

And for this we are very, very grateful to you.

Acts 24:3 TLB

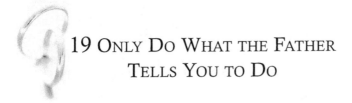

19 ONLY DO WHAT THE FATHER TELLS YOU TO DO

Jesus' modus operandi was to simply say and do whatever the Father commanded. If God didn't want it said, Jesus didn't say it. If the Father wanted something done, Jesus did it.

Consider acting like Jesus toward your mate. Give your mate permission at any time to ask you:

"Did the Father tell you to say that?"

"Did the Father tell you to do that?"

That question may be asked in the middle of a heated discussion or an angry outburst. That question may be asked whenever something is happening between the two of you that doesn't reflect God's purity, truth and character.

Consider this: Acting and speaking like the Father usually requires us to be patient, quick to listen, slow to speak, slow to anger and eager to surrender our rights instead of defending ourselves.

So often we believe we have the right in a marriage to say whatever we think or feel. But marriage isn't a license to freely treat the other person as we like. Marriage is a covenant to freely treat the other person in a manner that pleases God.

Try this: Give one another permission to interrupt any action or conversation that doesn't reflect God's character with one of the above questions.

I do nothing of myself; but as my Father taught me, I speak these things.

John 8:28-29

20 PRIZE YOUR MATE'S GIFTS AND TALENTS

"I never knew you could speak in front of a group," confessed the amazed wife. Her husband had just finished teaching some very significant truths which she had never heard him express.

In order to prize your mate's gifts, you must first know what they are. How do you discover those gifts and talents? First, go to the gifts listed in Romans 12, 1 Corinthians 12, Ephesians 4 and 1 Peter 4. Share with your mate the spiritual giftings you have seen in his life. Then ask your mate to tell you what spiritual gifts he has seen at work in your life. Or, tell your mate what spiritual gifts you believe God has given to you.

Next affirm one another's talents. Make a list of those talents from each other's perspective and experience. Begin to pray over that list of gifts and talents. Ask the Holy Spirit to continue to empower your mate in them.

Finally each of you select one gift and talent that you will affirm and pray specifically for continually each month. Focus on what you have selected both in prayer and affirmation. See how the Spirit increases both the depth and effectiveness of the gifts and talents in your marriage.

Try this: Each of you choose a gift which is not operating effectively in your life right now. Decide to ask God's Spirit to increase that gift. Pray together.

But earnestly desire the greater gifts.

1 Cor. 12:21

21 GO TO SLEEP RECONCILED

How often have you lost a night's rest because you went to bed angry? Anger isn't worth holding on to even for one night. Sleep doesn't mitigate your angry feelings. In fact, you may wake up angrier than you were before you went to bed.

Resolve your anger quickly. Unresolved anger can become the greatest threat to your marital harmony and peace. You are one flesh. Anger hurts you and your spouse. One of you may win an angry argument, but in winning out of anger, you both lose!

Repent quickly of any offense that you feel. Carrying unforgiveness, anger and offenses will bring division into your marriage and hinder God's Spirit from bringing healing to your hurts. Jesus commands us to forgive others. Repentance and forgiveness are not options; they are mandates.

Correct what you are saying or doing that brings strife, anger and conflict into your relationship. Ask your mate and the Lord, "What can I do or say to change so that God's love flows freely through me?"

Try this: When you are angry, set a time when both of you can honestly speak the truth in love.

Share your anger with "I" messages instead of "You" messages. Say, "I feel angry when _____." Don't say, "You make me angry when _____." Take responsibility for your own feelings.

Don't blame the other person for how you feel.

If you are angry, don't sin by nursing your grudge.
Don't let the sun go down with you still angry—get
over it quickly; for when you are angry, you give a
mighty foothold to the devil.   Eph. 4:26-27

22 FACE THE PROBLEM NOW

Many of us hate confrontation. In fact, we often embrace the myth that, "Time heals." The truth is that time never heals. Only God's wisdom, power and love can bring true healing into a conflict, problem or crisis. Instead of facing our problems now, we often procrastinate. We put off the financial problem until it becomes a crisis. We delay asking forgiveness until there's lasting hurt. We procrastinate setting boundaries and rules for our children until they get into trouble.

Life is filled with problem-solving. Ignoring our difficulties will not make them go away. It's time to be proactive and level the molehill now before it becomes a mountain.

Try this: When facing a problem, ask yourselves these three questions:

What is God's best for us in this situation?

How can we surrender our opinions and feelings to God's plans and directions for our lives?

What is a simple first step we can take to solve the problem?

Don't be afraid to ask for help. Pray. Seek godly counsel from those wise and mature in their faith. Trust God's Spirit to give you wisdom and discernment. Finally, listen to each other's hearts. Remember that the situation is the problem; your mate isn't the problem!

And now just as you trusted Christ to save you, trust him, too, for each day's problems; live in vital union with him.

Col. 2:6-7 TLB

22

23 PRAY;
GOD DOESN'T NEED YOUR HELP;
HE WANTS YOUR PRAYERS

God has all the power and ability necessary to change you or your mate. Truthfully, there is nothing you can do to change your mate. The only person you can change is yourself.

Your prayers become God's instrument of change in your marriage. How? By changing you! Instead of praying, "Oh God, change my mate." Start praying, "Oh God, change me!"

So, how can you pray for your spouse? Try praying this way:

Lord, open my mate's eyes to see You face to face. Open my mate's ears to hear You clearly. Open my mate's heart to receive all that You have to deposit in him. Empower my mate to become a willing, living sacrifice wholly dedicated to You. Amen.

Remember that God loves you too much to leave you the way you are. Prayer changes the one praying. Praying becomes the change agent in your marriage relationship.

Prayer is the language of spiritual intimacy between you and your partner. Share your deepest needs with each other and God through prayer.

Try this: Find an area in your relationship that both of you agree needs changing. Pray in agreement, surrendering that area to God and asking Him to totally change you.

Confess your trespasses to one another, and pray for one another, that you may be healed.

James 5:16

23

24 SPEND POSITIVE TIME TOGETHER DAILY

All of us have emotional banks. Gary Smalley talks about this in *Making Love Last Forever*. We make deposits in each other by doing and saying positive things. We make withdrawals from each other by doing and saying negative things.

Is your mate's emotional bank full, or is it overdrawn? We cannot make positive deposits into one another without spending time, one-on-one and face-to-face, with each other daily.

How much time are you willing to spend positively with your spouse each day? That means that in your positive time you cannot argue or discuss problems or crises. In that time you find ways to make positive deposits into each other's emotional banks. Find out what your mate enjoys doing with you and begin doing that daily. Of course, physical intimacy may be part of that time. But reading, praying, walking, sharing, holding hands, exercising, singing, worshiping and many other things can fill that time.

Try this: Choose a realistic amount of time you can spend together each day. Set that time and guard it intensely. No children. No phone. No TV. No distractions. Take time for just the two of you together…positively.

O my dove, in the clefts of the rock,
In the secret places of the cliff,
Let me see your face,
Let me hear your voice;
For your voice is sweet,
And your face is lovely.

Song 2:14

25 NEVER DEFEND YOURSELF

Excuses. Excuses. Excuses. You've heard people try to weasel out of a sticky situation with a feeble excuse. It would've been better for them and everyone else if they'd just admitted the mistake and gotten on with life.

Excuses in marriage are like a tomato that has a rotten spot. It may look good, but when you pick it up, your finger pokes right through. Yuck!

Defending yourself sets the stage for attempting to excuse your behavior. That's what an excuse is. Too often, though, the behavior cannot be excused because it was wrong!

Adam was the first recorded excuse-maker in the world when he told God, "The woman whom You gave to be with me, she gave me of the tree, and I ate" (Gen. 3:12). Adam's feeble attempt to justify what he'd done only drove him farther away from God. Likewise, when you try to excuse your actions, you are only driving yourself farther away from your spouse.

Try this: Next time you're caught in an embarrassing situation, instead of making excuses, just tell the truth. Avoid using blaming language and own up to what you've done. Stop trying to justify and instead begin to rectify. If you do this, you'll be amazed at how much easier it is to get past the problem and get on with life.

If God is your sure defense, then why do a poor job defending yourself?

To You, O my Strength, I will sing praises;
For God is my defense, My God of mercy.

Ps. 59:17

26 PARENT IN AGREEMENT

Children gifts from God. Furthermore, we know that it's God's will for married couples to have children. Scripture plainly tells us to "be fruitful and multiply" (Gen. 1:26-27), and that "Children's children are the crown of old men" (Prov. 17:6).

However, what if your children have problem after problem? What happens when one of your kids is rebellious or belligerent? What do you do then?

Studies show that the lowest point of marital happiness is during the teen years. Ask most parents of teenagers and they'll quickly agree. Not only are your kids going through tremendous changes in their lives, but you are too! And everyone knows that change is very uncomfortable.

To parent in agreement means that both spouses have agreed to boundaries, rules, and the consequences of disobedience before they present them to their children. They have already covered the ground of their own differences, paving the way for a unified approach.

Try this: Sit down with your spouse and discuss both of your philosophies of parenting. Make note of the differences and similarities of your approaches to discipline, rewards, boundaries and rules. Come into agreement beforehand about each of these areas. Clearly communicate the rules and consequences to your children. Finally, BE CONSISTENT in your discipline.

Can two walk together, unless they are agreed?

Amos 3:3

27 WINNING LOSES:
IF ONE WINS THE ARGUMENT, BOTH LOSE

"I told you so." Where does it stop? You know, the finger pointing. When is enough enough? What's the cost of being right all the time?

To say that conflict never happens in marriage is to deny the uniqueness of the individuals involved. Spouses bring their own pasts, wants, desires and expectations into the marriage, placing them on a collision course with one another—it's just a matter of time.

However, the test is not that there is no conflict; it's how the conflict is handled. Marriage is the proving ground of Christian devotion. No other human relationship provides the opportunity to grow in selflessness that marriage does.

It's possible to be angry without inviting a war. Conflict seeks to inflict pain, causes casualties and ultimately hurts the other person. Express your anger by taking responsibility for your feelings without blaming the other person.

Try this: Say to your mate, "I am angry about ___." Now be quick to listen and slow to speak. Remember that your object is to be understood, not to win an argument. Try to find a solution in which both of you win.

Let nothing be done through selfish ambition
or conceit, but in lowliness of mind
let each esteem others better than himself.
Let each of you look out not only for his own interests,
but also for the interests of others.

Phil. 2:3-4

28 Write Down God's Vision for Your Marriage

Your vision is bound by possibilities, time and space. But God's vision for your marriage has eternal significance and can move you from the realm of possibilities into the realm of impossibilities.

God's presence gives you the perspective and vision to see the lasting impact everything in your marriage you will possess. If whatever you do or say is birthed by God's vision for your marriage, then you will be on-purpose and will accomplish that which lasts forever.

So what is God's vision for both of you? The crucible of His vision for you both is rooted in Genesis 1:28, "Then God blessed them, and God said to them, "Be fruitful and multiply...." In your design and destiny, God envisioned that you would prosper and that your seed and seed's seed would inherit both natural and spiritual blessings from you. So God's vision goes far beyond just you. It's about your seed and your seed's seed.

God's presence will give you the eyes to see beyond the present into your destiny as a couple. Your household will be saved and will become a blessing to others. Your future will be anchored in God's power to enable you to flourish, multiply, walk in authority and take control of the circumstances around you.

Try this: Write down the vision God is birthing in your marriage. Complete this sentence: "Our future in God's hand will bear fruit and multiply through_____."

Then the LORD answered me and said: Write the vision and make it plain on tablets, that he may run who reads it.   Hab. 2:1

29 KEEP YOUR MARRIAGE VOW; YOU'RE IN A COVENANT, NOT A CONTRACT

"Contracts are made to be broken," the businessman advised me. I was appalled. But then I considered how most couples regard their marriage as a contract, not a covenant. What's the difference?

A contract has provisions for being broken.
A covenant is lasting.
A contract is a bilateral agreement.
A covenant is trilateral—God, husband and wife.
A contract makes provisions for termination.
A covenant lasts a lifetime.
A contract has terms and rules.
A covenant is based on relationship.
A contract protects one's rights.
A covenant surrenders rights to God.
A contract anticipates possible failure.
A covenant provides for success.
A contract initiates in good faith.
A covenant initiates in love.

People break contracts all the time. But God keeps spouses in covenant through His power, love and forgiveness.

Try this: Regard your marriage as a covenant, not a contract. Refuse to ever speak the "d" word to one another—divorce.

The LORD has been a witness between you
and the wife of your youth . . .
she is your companion and your wife by covenant.

Mal. 2:14 NAS

29

30 ENJOY SERENDIPITIES

A serendipity is an unplanned experience of joy. You can enjoy the unexpected. Marriage is full of unplanned experiences that can either unsettle you or enliven you.

Recently my wife and I unexpectedly found ourselves stranded in a strange city for 48 hours with no plans or expectations.

Wow, we had a great time together! Instead of trying our best to get out of there and return home, we counted each hour as a fresh experience of joy and discovery.

We rested. We enjoyed intimate time together. We explored. We talked and prayed. We planned and encouraged one another. We read to each other. We reveled in the joy of the unexpected.

Your serendipity may arrive as unplanned time, an unexpected visit from someone or a gift that has to be used now. Are you prepared to enjoy your serendipity?

Your serendipity may be a divine appointment or a missed opportunity to commune with God or entertain an angel unawares. It depends on you. Your response will determine your joy or your stress. Decide now that joy, not frustration, will greet your next serendipity.

Try this: Plan for the unexpected. Have a day each month just for the two of you to encounter whatever God has for that day. Plan your unplanned day to be a serendipity from God.

This is the day the LORD has made;
We will rejoice and be glad in it.

Ps. 118:24

31 ENJOY THE JOURNEY

"As soon as the baby is born, we will...."
"As soon as junior is out of diapers, we will...."
"When he moves out, we will...."
"After we pay off the debt, we must...."
"When we retire, we will...."

Some couples keep wishing their lives away. They can't enjoy the journey. They are always looking ahead to the next passage to the time they will take a vacation, enjoy one another, or do something special together.

We want to have goals, but not at the expense of missing the moment. We need destinations in life, but not at the risk of missing the journey. Couples who can't enjoy the journey always find themselves sacrificing relationships for goals and intimacy for quick fixes. Enjoying the journey is like a gallery of portraits that one can enjoy and ponder. Missing the journey is like trying to watch a movie on fast forward and really enjoying it. It's impossible.

Try this: Stop speeding through life like you're driving down an interstate. Take an alternate route. Pull off along the shoulder and take a walk among the wildflowers. Enjoy the daily walk of marriage. Remember it's a marathon, not a sprint.

Be very careful, then, how you live—not as unwise but as wise, making the most of every opportunity, because the days are evil.

Eph. 5:15 NIV

31

32 ALWAYS EXPECT GOD TO BE DOING SOMETHING NEW IN YOUR MARRIAGE

"I wish we could just have two weeks alike," moaned the frustrated husband.

Truthfully, the only constant in life is change. God is the God of the new. He is continually doing a new thing in your marriage.

New means change. God is changing you from the inside out. He's making you a new creation (2 Cor. 5:17). The same is true of marriage. Two people constantly becoming new will always bring new challenges and changes into a marriage relationship. New also means fresh. Expect something fresh in your marriage—fresh water to cleanse out the dirt of daily life and bring vitality to your spirit.

Expect fresh bread to feed upon from God's Word. Read the Word together daily to feed on God's fresh manna for you.

Welcome a fresh wind filling the sails of your marriage, empowering you to go to new places both naturally and spiritually. Marriage grows stale without God's newness bringing change and freshness on a daily basis.

Try this: Memorize a new Scripture together each week. Worship together with a new song, hymn or chorus. Find someone new to serve this week.

Behold, I will do a new thing,
Now it shall spring forth;
Shall you not know it?
I will even make a road in the wilderness
And rivers in the desert.

Is. 43:19

32

33 LEAVE AN INHERITANCE FOR YOUR CHILDREN

"I can't believe it. My kids are starting off where I left off. They have so much more now than we had when we started in marriage. It's just not fair," protested the selfish parents.

A bumper sticker common to the geographic area where we live reads, "I'm spending my kids' inheritance." How sad. Why would we want to bankrupt the next generation?

We are blessed to be a blessing. Of course, we want our children to start off better than we did. We have made progress through the years. Our desire is to launch them into a new level of spiritual and material prosperity. We leave our children...

A spiritual inheritance of household salvation in which each successive generation knows Jesus Christ as Lord and Savior.

A relational inheritance for covenant marriage and godly parenting.

A communal inheritance of faith in being a member of the body of Christ.

A material inheritance not just of wealth but of how to create wealth and sow it into the work of God's kingdom.

A parental inheritance which has broken generational curses and initiated generations of blessing.

A stewardship inheritance so that our children know how to serve Christ and others while being stewards, not possessors, of all the provisions He has given them.

Try this: With your spouse, sit down and write the epitaph on your memorial.

Write what you would like your children to remember about you.

A good man leaves an inheritance
to his children's children.

Prov. 13:22

34 MEASURE GROWTH BY FRUIT, NOT JUST STUFF

Each time we moved during our marriage, we couldn't believe how much stuff we had accumulated. Nonetheless, we could not measure our impact based on the number of moving boxes we had added since the last move. Rather, we had to measure growth by other criteria, such as:

Had we changed for the better?

Was the fruit of the Spirit more evident in our marriage and family than before?

Was our relationship with Jesus Christ more passionate and loving?

Had anyone around us been saved, healed or delivered?

Are we growing more deeply in God's presence and purposes for our marriage?

Fruit always has two components—substance and seed. Substance is what feeds us now in the journey. Seed is what is sown into our children and others to bring a harvest in the kingdom.

Robert H. Schuller often quips, "You can count the seeds in an apple, but you can never count the number of apples in a seed." Marriage is more than accumulating stuff; it's sowing seed into the lives of others that produces more fruit and finally much fruit (read John 15).

Try this: Sit down together as a couple and review the last year, five years and ten years. Answer the questions from the criteria listed above about each span of time.

So God created man in His own image;
in the image of God He created him;
male and female He created them.
Then God blessed them, and God said to them,
"Be fruitful and multiply...."

Gen. 1:27-28

35 Purpose
to be Married for Life

"Until death do us part," sounds archaic and traditional. However, that's exactly what we expect a covenant to be: lifelong.

I was standing at the grocery counter as the twenty-something clerk rang up my groceries. My golf shirt read, "Married for Life."

"I'm so sorry," she commented. I was taken back. I couldn't believe my ears. She was actually feeling bad for me because I was married for life.

"Why are you sorry?" I asked.

"You are stuck with the same person forever. What happens if you get tired of that person?" she mused.

Sadly, this young woman had a cultural bias against marriage. Too many think of marriage as a convenience instead of a commitment for life. If they should get tired of the relationship, they simply trade the present mate in for a new one, much like trading cars.

We need to love one another the same way that God loves us—forever. God loves us no matter what the circumstance or the convenience. He never gives up on us. In loving our mates, we say to them, "I will love you forever!"

Try this: With your mate decide that your marriage is for life, not for the moment. Discuss what you may be doing together five years from now, twenty or even thirty years from now. See yourselves spending all of life loving each other.

"Yes, I have loved you with an everlasting love."

Jer. 31:3

37

36 RELEASE YOUR MATE TO BE ALL GOD CREATED HER TO BE

Whatever we try to control or dominate in marriage, we will ultimately destroy. One of the deadly cancers that eats away at marital harmony is control.

Are you a controlling and dominating spouse? Do you find yourself correcting almost everything your mate says? Do you have to know everywhere your mate is going and everything your mate is doing all of the time?

Every new creation in Christ has infinite potential. Your mate is filled with gifts, talents and untapped potential that will bless both you and your family.

Remember, marriage is not about you; it's about you mate, your seed and your seed's seed. The tighter you try to smother who your mate is and what your mate does, the farther you will push your spouse away from you.

Affirm your mate's gifts. See your mate the way God's sees him—overflowing with possibilities and abundant purpose in life. Remember that your mate doesn't belong to you. He belongs to Christ.

Try this: Read 1 Corinthians 12 and Romans 12 with your spouse. Ask each other to identity some of the gifts you each possess. Pray this prayer over your spouse, "I release God's full potential and giftings in your life to be used for His glory. Amen."

There are many ways in which God works in our lives, but it is the same God who does the work in and through all of us who are His.

1 Cor. 12:6-7

37 SAY, "HOW MAY I SERVE YOU?"

Mutual submission in marriage is often more difficult for men than women. Raised in a male-dominated culture, men often expect women to serve them. But Ephesians 5 describes something quite different.

Remember that there is no division in the original biblical manuscript designated by subhead, punctuation, chapter or verse. So the traditional subheading between Ephesians 5:21 and Ephesians 5:24 defining the next section as "Christian Marriage" has been inserted there by editors, not by Paul.

When we are filled by the Spirit (5:18), we will find ourselves worshiping the Lord and serving one another (5:21). The best example in life of such spiritual service is a marriage in which both husband and wife serve one another in love.

In fact, the service that the husband renders is sacrificial. He is called to lay down his life for his wife as Christ lays down His life for His bride, the Church. So the overriding attitude of marriage is "submitting to one another in the fear of God."

If both husband and wife are servants, then one will not rule over the other, making unrealistic demands or expecting unattainable tasks. With both husband and wife serving one another, love replaces expectations, and demands give way to service.

Try this: Get up in the morning asking your mate, "How may I serve you?" Go out of your way to meet your spouse's needs. Develop a servant heart for your spouse.

Submit to one another out of reverence for Christ.
                                                    Eph. 5:21 NIV

38 Stay On-Purpose

L ife is filled with distractions. Your marriage will be pulled in scores of different directions. It's so easy to chase after good ideas instead of God ideas.

Remember Abraham and Sarah? They had a good idea. God had promised them a baby boy in their old age. But waiting on God's purpose took too long, and they were impatient. So they took things into their own hands.

Sarah gave Abraham her maidservant, Hagar; with Hagar they birthed Ishmael. Ishmael seemed like such a good idea, but he wasn't God's idea.

God's idea was Isaac. But Isaac required Abraham and Sarah to stay on purpose with God. Isaac was born in God's time and God's way. Is your marriage on purpose in birthing Isaacs or off purpose in birthing Ishmaels?

Staying on purpose requires faith. Faith trusts God. Faith hears the incredible, sees the invisible and does the impossible. Without faith we merely hear the credible, see the visible and do the possible.

Keep your marriage on-purpose by trusting God with your actions, decisions and directions.

Try this: Look at every decision you make in light of God's presence and purposes for your marriage. Ask yourselves, "Is that on purpose?" Refuse to do anything that isn't on-purpose for your lives.

To everything there is a season,
A time for every purpose under heaven.

Eccl. 3:1

40

39 Know That Your Past Doesn't Determine Your Future

Every marriage has past mistakes and failures, but to dwell on the past destroys a marriage. It's time to forget the past and move forward with God.

God is saying to your marriage right now,
Do not remember the former things,
Nor consider the things of old.
Behold, I will do a new thing,
Now it shall spring forth;
Shall you not know it?
I will even make a road in the wilderness
And rivers in the desert."   Is. 43:18-19

Constantly bringing up the past will continue to bring strife and conflict into your marriage. When you rehearse the past, you become its slave. Sink your mate's past mistakes into a sea of forgetfulness, and post a "No Fishing" sign there. Let go of the past so you can walk into God's future for your marriage.

God determines your future. Let Him lead you into new attitudes, words and behaviors toward each other. The past words of death must die. The past destructive actions must cease. The past hurtful attitudes must perish. It's time for God's new ways in your marriage. Try this: Agree never to bring up past mistakes and failures in your discussions. If one of you should do so, develop a sign, a look between the two of you that immediately reminds you to stop talking about the past.

Our heavenly Father will forgive you if you forgive
those who sin against you.
                              Matt. 6:14 TLB

41

40 FACE THE PROBLEM

None of us ever arrives in marriage. We are always growing and learning. How does that happen?

Learn from each other. My wife teaches me much about marriage, herself, family, living in the world and walking with Christ. Learn from your spouse.

Study the Word. The Holy Spirit teaches us all truth through Scripture. Study the Word together at home and at church.

Listen to others. Those around us have much wisdom and experience in marriage. Find a small group of couples who want to grow in their marriages. Form a life group, cell group or other small group study to learn together.

Read good books. An abundance of excellent materials has been written on marriage. Read Christian books aloud to each other.

Get help when you need it. At times, we may need to be teachable in counseling. There's nothing wrong with working through your problems with another skilled person.

Develop a teachable spirit. Put aside pride. Ask questions. Remember that you are a student, a disciple for a lifetime. As we learn together, our marriages grow and become more intimate. Our relationship with God also deepens.

Try this: Find a good Christian book on marriage. Read it to each other. Discuss it together. Learn and grow as a couple.

Be diligent to present yourself approved to God, a worker who does not need to be ashamed, rightly dividing the word of truth. 2 Tim. 2:15

41 BE TEACHABLE

" Let's talk about this problem right now and stop putting it off," pleaded the husband. Let's face it. Sometimes we procrastinate until a small problem becomes a major wall in marriage.

Sometimes, it's wise to set aside the discussion of a heated issue until you can talk about it calmly. When that's the case, make an appointment with your mate. "I can't talk at this moment. Can we discuss it at _____." In other words, give yourself and your spouse some time to cool down.

However, never put off a problem for an extended period of time. The ideal is to face the problem and to deal with it now. The passage of time never makes a problem disappear.

It may take weeks, months or even years to solve a problem. Solutions aren't instant in marriage. But starting now can greatly diffuse future conflicts and trials in your marriage.

Now is the time to face the problem. Now is the time to pray. Now is the time to listen to one another. Now is the time to get help. Now is the time to develop an action plan.

Try this: Decide to talk about a problem when both of you are rested, not hungry and when there are no distractions. Set an appointment to talk.

"I will rise now," I said, "And go about the city; In the streets and in the squares I will seek the one I love."

Song 3:2

42 LEARN EACH OTHER'S NONVERBAL LANGUAGE

What we don't say to each other speaks volumes. Much communication is nonverbal. Ponder this list and reflect on how your spouse communicates in each of the following nonverbal ways:

- **Facial expression**. Eye contact and how your mate uses her face to communicate reveals much about what's happening inside.
- **Tone of voice**. It's not what we say that often causes conflict; it's how we say it.
- **Body language**. Observe the way your mate is sitting in a chair. Are arms and legs crossed or open to receive? Is your spouse facing you or turned away? How does your mate gesture with her hands?
- **Appearance**. How is your spouse dressing? What she wears and when she wears it communicates how she is feeling about the moment. Notice your mate's grooming or makeup.
- **Scent**. Notice how your mate smells. Do with perfume or cologne what your mate prefers.
- **Touch**. Much of what we communicate is through touch (or the lack of it).

Try this: Discuss with your mate other ways the two of you communicate nonverbally and what they mean.

My sister, my spouse; You have ravished my heart
With one look of your eyes, With one link of your
necklace.   Song 4:9

43 LISTEN BEFORE YOU SPEAK

Paul counseled Timothy to be quick to listen, slow to speak and slow to anger. That's great counsel for marriages.

First hear all that your spouse is saying. Paraphrase back to your mate what you heard to be certain you understood what was said. Share the feelings that you are perceiving from what he has shared.

Next you may describe the behavior you observe in what he is doing as he communicates. Often your spouse is unaware of negative body language when he is communicating.

Then disclose how you are feeling. Don't blame your mate for your feelings. Simply share honestly.

Finally speak from your heart and be calm. Refuse to let anger take control of your actions or words. Even when you feel angry, speak the truth out of love instead of anger.

Remember that a hasty response will bring forth words that you may later regret.

Try this: The next time your spouse is communicating to you in a very angry way, respond in love; don't react in anger.

Everyone should be quick to listen,
slow to speak and slow to become angry.

James 1:19

44 REFUSE TO DUMP ON YOUR SPOUSE

What's dumping? Dumping takes all your trashy negative feelings and uses your spouse as a garbage can. Dumping may help you feel better, but it transfers your negative feelings and attitudes to someone else.

I remember a time when I would come home and tell my wife all my negative feelings about a certain person. When I finished dumping, I felt better but she would then feel negative toward that person. A.W. Tozer suggested an important spiritual vow, "Never pass anything on about anyone that would hurt them."

That vow includes your spouse. Instead of dumping, try debriefing. Debriefing requires both mates to agree on how and what they will share with each other.

Debriefing...

Takes responsibility for your own feelings. Instead of blaming others for how you feel, you share what you feel and how you can heal from your hurts and overcome negativity and offense.

Agrees that you will cast your cares on the Lord. Instead of being burdened by your problems, you turn to God with them.

Prays in order to receive God's perspective. Wisdom comes from God. Wisdom is how God sees the problem. Prayer helps you see the situation from God's perspective.

Acts in faith trusting God to change you and release His potential and healing in you.

Try this: Debrief one another the next time one of you brings home a hurt.

When others are happy, be happy with them.
If they are sad, share their sorrow.

Rom. 12:15 TLB

45 UNDERSTAND BEFORE YOU TRY TO FIX IT

Mates often assume they know what's wrong before they really understand what's happening inside their spouses. Remember that the presenting problem is rarely the real problem.

Assume nothing. Ask your spouse to explain before you leap into a rescue or a fix of the situation.

Remember that you are called to be your spouse's mate, not his savior or rescuer. Too often husbands, in particular, want to fix their wives' feelings, hurts and concerns. All the wife may really need is someone to listen with empathy.

Understanding comes through listening and asking your spouse to explain. Avoid rushing to a solution until both of you understand each other.

Understanding rarely occurs if you leap into the problem, trying to fix the problem before you understand everything your mate needs.

Try this: Ask your spouse what he needs instead of assuming you know. Take time to explain what's happening inside of you and understand what's happening inside your spouse.

Share each other's troubles and problems, and so obey our Lord's command. If anyone thinks he is too great to stoop to this, he is fooling himself. He is really a nobody.

Gal. 6:2-3 TLB

48

46 BE PRESENCE-DRIVEN

A presence-driven marriage understands that God's presence births purposes, God's purposes birth plans and God's plans birth productivity. What happens in your marriage must be determined by God's Spirit. Otherwise, it is destined to be temporary instead of lasting.

God's presence births purpose in your marriage. A purpose has a time and season. Stepping into a purpose too soon can cause it to be stillborn. Holding on to an old purpose after its season is like trying to preserve manna. It smells.

God's purpose in His timing and for His glory will birth abundant plans. So if one plan fails, God will birth another.

God's plans always birth productivity. In other words, good fruit arises out of God's plans. That fruit always conforms in quality to the fruit of the Spirit—love, joy, peace, patience, kindness, goodness, faithfulness, gentleness and self-control (Gal. 5:22-23).

Try this: Before moving forward, pray with your spouse concerning God's next purpose and plan for your marriage. Be certain to birth what God desires, not what the two of you simply think may be a good idea.

The LORD replied, "My Presence will go with you, and
I will give you rest."
Then Moses said to him,
"If your presence does not go with us,
do not send us up from here."

Ex. 33:14-15 NIV

47 BREAK PAST CURSES

We were driving with a team to lead a marriage seminar in another state. As the team prayed about the seminar, God spoke to our hearts. God revealed, "Couples cannot receive all I have for them in their marriages as long as the past keeps them in bondage."

As we continued in prayer, the enemy's attack on marriage became very clear. The enemy was attacking through past open doors and curses involving:

Divorce – Spouses who personally have been through divorce, or have family or close friends who are divorced, have an open door from the past; this tempts fear and anxiety to consider divorce when problems arise.

Abuse – Spouses who have been sexually, emotionally, spiritually or physically abused in the past have open doors for attack in that area of their marriages.

Addiction – Spouses or family members who were chemically, emotionally or physically addicted are open to attacks from this curse.

Abandonment – Spouses who have experienced abandonment, detachment, rejection or apathy from a parent or guardian, particularly a father, have that curse to contend with in marriage.

Religion – Spouses who have been in a false religion, paganism, the occult, new age, secret societies and legalism find that they are attacked in those areas in their present marriage.

Try this: If you or your mate have any open doors from the past curses, pray this prayer together: Almighty God, we agree together in the name of Jesus the Christ to renounce the works of the devil and to break the curse of _____ from our past, through the blood of Jesus Christ. Amen.

Remember that Satan's first and ongoing attack is against marriage (read Gen. 2:23-3:8). Shut every past door and break every curse or bondage the enemy may try to bring against your marriage.

> *Christ redeemed us from the curse of the law by*
> *becoming a curse for us, for it is written:*
> *"Cursed is everyone who is hung on a tree."*
> *He redeemed us in order that the blessing given to*
> *Abraham might come to the Gentiles through Christ*
> *Jesus, so that by faith we might receive the promise of*
> *the Spirit.*

Gal. 3:13-14 NIV

48 GOD CHANGES; YOU ENCOURAGE

One of the most common prayers that spiritually immature mates pray concerning their spouses is, "God change my mate."

The prayer of a spiritually mature husband or wife is, "God change me!"

You cannot change your spouse. All your cajoling, nagging, criticisms and manipulations will not change your spouse. Besides, what you want changed may not be the real need for growth in your mate's feelings, attitudes, opinions or behaviors.

Encouragement works wonders to create a desire for change in your mate's life. Encourage her strengths. Look for her gifts and talents. Affirm at every turn.

Change always happens from within. External pressure to change—a spouse or another person trying to force change—simply doesn't work. Besides, when change comes from God's Spirit, the power to grow in that change also comes from God.

Try this: Ask God to show you where you need to change in order to grow in your marriage. When God answers, pray, "Lord, I'm willing." If you cannot pray that, then pray, "Lord, I'm willing to be made willing."

Therefore encourage one another and build each other up, just as in fact you are doing.

1 Thess. 5:11 NIV

49 Make Marriage
a Three-Fold Cord—
the Two of You and God

What's at the center of your marriage? The love you share? Your children? Money, homes and possessions? Your hopes, dreams and aspirations?

What?

Covenant marriage puts Jesus in the center. Without God at the center, your marriage will never become "one flesh."

God keeps you together even when you don't "feel in love." God's Spirit heals hurts and breaks bondages. God at the center of your marriage empowers you to live to your fullest potential both as a couple and as persons.

God is at the center of your marriage when you pray, study the Scriptures, seek His presence, worship, give, witness and live a holy life.

God is not at the center of your marriage when you ignore His Spirit as you make decisions, solve problems and live life your way instead of His.

Try this: Agree upon where you will worship together. Set aside time to pray together. Seek God's presence as you read Scripture and fill the atmosphere of your home with worship.

And a threefold cord is not quickly broken.

Eccl. 4:12

50 PRAISE GOD
AS YOUR SOURCE

Some wives believe that their husbands' jobs are the sources for their families. Some husbands' have made their wives their sources of income to make ends meet.

When we look to each other as our source, we will always come up short. No person can ever be our source for provision, for all of our needs, or all of the love we require in life.

Our mates are not God; God alone is our source. When a couple turns totally to God to supply all their needs, then jobs, money and provision are put into their proper perspectives.

God is the source for our finances and those of our children. Consequently we learn to turn to God when our family has needs. Certainly God may use one of us to supply a need in our marriage or family. But God has many ways to meet our needs. He can use others to work miracles that will meet our needs. We have but to ask Him!

Recognizing God as our source leads us to an attitude of gratitude in our lives. Instead of focusing on our lack, we focus our love and attention on the only One who can meet our needs.

Try this: With your spouse, write down all the needs that God is supplying in your marriage and family. Then spend time praising Him and giving Him thanks for being your source.

And my God shall supply all your need according to
His riches in glory by Christ Jesus. Now to our God
and Father be glory forever and ever. Amen.

Phil. 4:19-20

51 PRAY FOR YOUR SPOUSE

Praying for your spouse is the most effective action you can take to help your mate grow spiritually and relationally. So, how do we pray for a spouse?

Agreement. Pray for your mate's needs. Keep a prayer list. Regularly pray through the needs list.

Intercession. Pray with your spouse. Agree in prayer for whatever is on your hearts.

Praise and Thanksgiving. Give thanks. Praise and thank God for all that your spouse is and does. Give thanks for both gifts and talents.

Protection. Place a hedge around your spouse (Job 1:10). Pray God's protection around your spouse. Cover your mate with the protecting blood of Jesus Christ which nullifies every attack of any enemy.

Confession. Confess and repent. If there are any sins that you both have committed as one flesh, go to God confessing and repenting of those sins. If we confess, God promises to forgive (1 John 1:9).

Of all that you can spiritually give your mate, prayer is the greatest gift. Pray without ceasing for your mate and watch God change both of you for the better. Try this: Pray through the prayers suggested above daily. Keep a prayer journal recording both what you prayed and how God answered your prayers.

Confess your trespasses to one another, and pray for one another, that you may be healed.

James 5:16

52 PRAY TOGETHER TO HEAR FROM GOD

Prayer is the language of spiritual intimacy. In prayer, we open our hearts to God and each other. Self-defense is abandoned and vulnerability is embraced when couples pray together. When couples pray together they come into agreement, often in areas which previously divided them and created conflict between them. How is such agreement and unity in prayer accomplished?

First, we agree to surrender our thoughts to God's thoughts. We release our ways and surrender to His ways. We stop pushing to implement our purposes and begin to wait patiently in His presence.

Next, we pray together, not to persuade God to agree with our perspective, but rather to receive His wisdom and guidance. As couples pray together they stop seeking to get God on "my side." Praying together doesn't ask, "God, are you on my side and against my mate?" Rather we pray together so that both of us may join Him.

Finally, praying together brings us into a posture of receiving and listening instead of telling God what we want or need. In other words, when couples pray together they want to hear from God instead of preach to each other.

Try this: Instead of coming to God with a list, try this time to come to God with open hearts and minds, and receive whatever He wants for your marriage. Use your time praying together in order to hear from God for your marriage.

They raised their voices together in prayer to God.

Acts 4:24 NIV

53 Pray Together Often

Too often we only pray together when there's a crisis or deep need. We wait until we can go no further without God, and then we throw ourselves onto His mercy, hoping for relief from our dilemma instead of restoration.

We want our problems solved by Him more than we desire His presence and guiding Spirit in our lives.

Praying together often keeps us close to one another and to God. Spiritual intimacy in marriage requires that we come together with God to really be "one flesh."

This meeting with God in prayer invites both His presence and His transforming power into our lives. So often when we pray together we find our marriage being constantly changed in His presence.

So what hinders us from praying together? We become so distracted by what we see that we fail to seek the invisible. We become so involved in ourselves that we abandon others, including our mates and God. We become so busy doing things that we miss out on becoming like Christ.

Try this: Decide that you will pray together each day. Let prayer come as dialogue with God and each other in the flow of everything you do. Pray together as you drive, eat, discuss and go through your day.

They all joined together constantly in prayer . . .

Acts 1:14 NIV

54 SOW BLESSING
INTO OTHER MARRIAGES

We reap what we sow. As we sow blessings into the marriages of others, our marriages grow deeper and more intimate.

We have discovered this in our own marriage. Every time we lead a marriage seminar with a group of couples and singles our marriage grows and we learn more about God and ourselves.

Whenever we help another couple, we mature in our own marital relationship. Whenever we pray for other marriages, our own marriage reaps a harvest of the Spirit's fruit.

Always focusing on our own marriage makes us selfish and self-centered. Giving to others our time, resources and gifts allows us to release what we have as blessings into the lives of others.

When fellowshipping with another couple, ask them, "How is your marriage and family? What wonderful things do you see God doing in and through you?" Let them share instead of selfishly dominating the conversation talking only about your marriage. Try this: Ask God to show you couples into whom you can sow blessings of resources, wisdom, spiritual gifts and time so that God can use you to bless others.

And let us not get tired of doing what is right, for after a while we will reap a harvest of blessing if we don't get discouraged and give up. That's why whenever we can we should always be kind to everyone, and especially to our Christian brothers.

Gal. 6:9-10 TLB

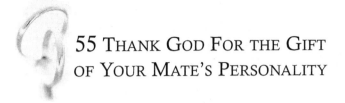

55 Thank God For the Gift of Your Mate's Personality

Often couples are initially attracted to one another by the unique personality of the other person. As time passes, however, the very uniqueness that attracted them becomes an irritant that threatens to divide and create strife.

Our personalities are often the sandpaper that God uses to smooth our mates' rough edges. We have observed how the irritation of sand can produce a pearl in an oyster. God is producing something precious in your marriage as your personalities "rub against" one another.

Value your mate's extroversion while your spouse respects your introversion.

Learn from a spouse's visionary preferences as that mate benefits from your focus on details.

Benefit from your spouse's feelings and emotion when you can get beyond your thoughts and logic.

Enjoy a mate's spontaneity even as your spouse will be helped by your organization and structure.

Try this: Take a personality inventory or temperament survey. A valuable resource is *Please Understand Me II* by David Keirsey. Share with your mate the traits you cherish and value in his or her personality.

Accept one another, then, just as Christ accepted you, in order to bring praise to God.

Rom. 15:7 NIV

56 GET OVER IT

A close friend just gave me a mug with "Get Over It" inscribed on the side. My wife gave me a sign for my counseling office years ago that read, "Get over it." So what is the *it*?

The *it* we must get over in marriage is anger. Release anger. Unresolved anger destroys marriage.

We don't release anger by blasting or hurting our mates. We don't get over anger by dumping on our mates. Try this:

We release anger by...

Taking responsibility for our own feelings, sharing honestly in love.

Allowing God to replace anger with forgiveness.

Believing the best instead of the worst about our mates.

Deciding that I can change even if my spouse doesn't.

Setting appropriate boundaries so that what caused the anger doesn't happen again.

Becoming calm instead of agitated.

Acting assertively not aggressively.

Admitting I was wrong in whatever part of the problem I created.

Knowing that my spouse is not the enemy.

Valuing the relationship more than being right.

Recognizing that my perceptions may not be reality.

Wanting both of us to win instead of me winning as my spouse loses.

Understanding that the battle is not against flesh and blood.

The time has come when we must decide as a couple to make "getting over it" our first priority whenever anger seeks to erode our covenant relationship.

Be angry, and do not sin: do not let the sun go down on your wrath, nor give place to the devil.

Eph. 4:26-27

57 Say "I was Wrong" When You are Wrong

The three hardest words to say in marriage are, "I was wrong." We try to defend ourselves or excuse our sin. A.W. Tozer's vow is helpful here: Never defend yourself.

God is our sure defense. Why would we choose to defend ourselves when God can bring His infinite resources and strength to our side?

However, many times our defense becomes a series of excuses that cannot replace true confession and repentance. The most direct path toward healing hurts in marriage is repentance.

Once you've admitted guilt, ask for forgiveness. Then quit doing or saying the hurtful thing. Allow yourself to forget the offense. Ask your mate to forget it also so that it's never brought up again.

Remember that even the slightest responsibility for hurt should be admitted. You don't have to be totally wrong to confess. Repent of any part you had in causing pain or hurt.

Try this: Say, "I was wrong," before you are caught. Admit to whatever part of being wrong you are responsible for.

Confess your trespasses to one another, and pray for one another, that you may be healed.

James 5:16

58 Confess Quickly; Repent Thoroughly and Sincerely

Don't procrastinate. The longer hurt lingers the deeper the wound and the harder it is for healing to come.

Sure it's hard to confess right when you hurt your mate. But confession is empowered by walking in the light. You are walking in the light and fellowshipping with Jesus. As soon as you sin, the Holy Spirit shows you what that sin is.

You know when you sin either in words or actions. You know when you have hurt your mate the moment you do it, so why not repent right away? Don't give the seeds of hurt a chance to grow. When you repent thoroughly, ask for forgiveness, being as specific as possible. For example, "I ask you to forgive me for _____." When you need to repent, and yet procrastinate, consider all the bad things that can happen:

- Your spouse is hurt or offended.
- You carry guilt around for days or weeks.
- Your marriage relationship stagnates.
- Your work suffers.
- Your prayer life dries up.
- Your relationship with God is hindered.

Try this: Give your mate permission to ask for your repentance at any time and in any situation.

But if we walk in the light as he is in the light, we have fellowship with one another, and the blood of Jesus Christ his Son cleanses us from all sin.

1 John 1:7-8

59 FORGIVE; IT'S MARRIAGE'S BALM FOR HEALING HURTS

Why is it so difficult to forgive our spouses? Here are some of the excuses I have heard:

"He should have known better than to do that and should never have done that."

"He really won't accept my forgiveness."

"I don't want to forgive right away. I want for him to feel guilty for a while and pay for what he's done."

"I have the right to feel angry and hurt for a while."

"I don't have to forgive until he repents."

"I've already had to forgive him for this too many times before."

"Forgiving him now lets him off the hook too soon. It's just cheap grace."

No matter how justified the excuse may seem, the truth is that all these excuses are prideful disobedience.

Not forgiving another person carries serious consequences. Christ commands us to forgive. Holding on to unforgiveness seriously damages your relationship with God as well as with your spouse (Matt. 6:14-15).

Try this: As soon as you feel hurt, offended or angry, forgive your spouse immediately. Share your feelings and speak the truth in love.

Jesus said to him, I do not say to you, up to seven times, but up to seventy times seven.

Matt. 18:22-23

60 PRAY SCRIPTURE
WITH EACH OTHER

"I don't know how to pray for or with my spouse," confessed a frustrated husband. Coming up with the right words may be difficult, especially for men who often have a private prayer life they are reluctant to share with their wives. An abundance of passages exist throughout the Bible that can be prayed with or over your spouse. The most common way to pray is to substitute your spouse's name for the personal pronoun in the text. For example, "The Lord is _____'s shepherd; ____shall not want."

Here is a list of great passages to pray with and for each other:

Numbers 6 – Praying blessing
Deuteronomy 28 – Praying prosperity
Psalm 23 – Praying nurture
Psalm 51 – Praying repentance
Psalm 91 – Praying protection
Psalm 103 – Praying praise and healing
Matthew 6 – Praying the Lord's prayer
1 Corinthians 13 – Praying love
Ephesians 1 – Praying grace and understanding
Ephesians 3 – Praying the indwelling of Christ
2 Peter 1 – Praying maturity

Try this: Each week find a new verse or a passage of Scripture you can prayer over or with your mate.

We give thanks to the God and Father of our Lord
Jesus Christ, praying always for you.

Col. 1:3

61 REFUSE OFFENSE

John Brevere aptly reminds us that offense is "the bait of Satan." Don't take the bait.

Here's how the bait of offense works in marriage. Your spouse says or does something hurtful. You feel hurt and pain. At that moment, the enemy whispers, "You have the right to be offended. Get angry. Get back. Get even. Stay hurt. Don't forgive."

At this point all that's really happened is a feeling and a temptation. Your next step makes all the difference. It's called your response.

Feelings are not right or wrong; responses are right or wrong. Feelings are simply emotional triggers within our souls. How we handle our feelings makes all the difference. We can choose to respond with hate or love, forgiveness or unforgiveness, peace or war.

Your response determines whether you take Satan's bait or resist it. Remember that his bait is a trap designed to steal your joy or love, destroy intimacy or even kill your relationship. The enemy can only gain a foothold in your marriage through offense. And you choose whether to take the bait or not.

Try this: The next time you are tempted to become offended with your spouse say out loud, "Get behind me, Satan, in Jesus' name."

Therefore submit to God.
Resist the devil and he will flee from you.
Draw near to God and He will draw near to you.

James 4:7-8

62 GIVE YOUR SPOUSE UNDIVIDED ATTENTION

One of the most common complaints we hear from wives in particular is that their husbands seem to be "somewhere else" when they are talking to them. Imagine that—a husband whose mind is drifting as his wife talks! It happens frequently.

Now it is true that when it comes to talking to their mates, on a daily basis, most wives have thousands more words to say than do their husbands. Nonetheless, one of the greatest gifts we can give each other when we're together is our undivided attention, even if we are tired of hearing the other person.

Giving your spouse your undivided attention communicates acceptance, love, caring and affirmation to her. Likewise not giving your undivided attention communicates apathy, indifference and lack of affection.

Try this: Here are some failsafe ways to ensure each other's undivided attention:

- Turn off the TV, CD player or computer.
- Shut off the phone, beeper or cell phone.
- Withdraw for the moment from children.
- Get alone together in a private place.
- Sit or stand face-to-face.
- Make eye contact.
- Focus your thoughts on the other person, not on something else.

I hope to come to you and speak face to face, that our joy may be full.

2 John: 12

63 BE A BURDEN BEARER, NOT A BURDEN

One spouse confessed, "I hate going home at the end of my work day. Everything there is so heavy. My mate is just waiting for me to listen to all the day's burdens."

It's irrational to believe that we must be upset by the problems of others. Being a burden bearer doesn't mean feeling upset about your spouse's burdens. Rather, bearing burdens involves helping a mate take those cares and problems to the Lord. How does that happen? We bear each other's burdens by:

- Debriefing each other, not dumping on one another.
- Listening without trying to diagnose or fix the burden.
- Caring with empathy instead of sympathy.
- Responding with joy and faith instead of despair and doubt.
- Focusing our attention on the problem-solver, Jesus, instead of the problem.
- Praying together.
- Crying and laughing together.
- Validating one another's feelings.
- Comforting one another.

Try this: After sharing burdens, take them in prayer to Jesus and release them instead of dwelling on them.

Therefore comfort each other and edify one another, just as you also are doing.

1 Thess. 5:11

64 GUARD YOUR HEART AND YOUR SENSES

Be careful to guard your heart and your senses, which are doorways through which both good and evil can enter. If you open the door to iniquity, then you are giving permission to the enemy to plunder your marriage relationship.

How then do we guard our hearts and senses? Here are some simple safeguards for both:

- Don't subscribe to premium movie channels or any channels that would show pornography.
- Filter out all temptation to look at porno on your computer.
- Refuse to watch "R"-rated films.
- Reject any music that is sexually suggestive or violent.
- Dress modestly.
- Don't put yourself in a compromising situation with a member of the opposite gender who isn't your mate.
- Refuse to look upon, touch or listen to anything that is unclean.
- Take every thought captive.

Temptations abound in the world around us. It's our responsibility to guard our hearts and senses from anything unclean.

Try this: Clean your house. Get rid of anything unclean in your physical and spiritual house.

*Or do you not know that your body is the temple
of the Holy Spirit who is in you, whom you have from
God, and you are not your own?*

1 Cor. 6:19

65 HUSBAND, GO FIRST TO BATTLE FOR AND PROTECT YOUR WIFE

Husbands are warriors; wives are nurturers. As such, husband, part of being "the head of the wife" is being the protector of the wife.

The husband as the head is like being the point of a spear. The spear's point goes first into battle and mortally wounds the enemy. Husband, if you desire to be the head of your marriage and family, then start going first.

Husband, go first into prayer.

Go first into worship.

Go first to work in providing for your family.

Go first in leading family devotions.

Go first into blessing your wife and children.

Go first into God's new thing.

Go first into love and pleasing your wife.

Go first into breaking curses.

Go first into God's presence.

Go first into studying and teaching God's Word in your family.

Try this: Take the initiative in love, prayer, affirmation and worship this week. See the positive impact this will make on your marriage.

For the husband is the head of the wife as Christ is the head of the church, his body, of which he is the Savior.

Eph. 5:23 NIV

71

66 SERVE AND WORSHIP GOD TOGETHER

As one flesh, it's so important to share worship and ministry together. So often at church, families are split apart. The wife goes in one direction, the husband in another, and the children disappear with their friends.

The problem with this becomes apparent; churches often segment families instead of unifying them. It's so important in marriage to find time to worship and serve God together.

Find a ministry that both of you can share together, and find a place of discipleship so that both of you can grow together. A small group or marriage class for couples may be one place for you to grow together.

Serving the Lord in the church should bring you together, not separate you. Some couples sacrifice their marriages on the altar of ministry. Don't let that happen to you.

Discover a place where you can minister together, such as in leading a group, praying with people together after a service, in a visitation ministry or singing together on a worship team or in choir.

Try this: Make a schedule for a month of all the times you worship or are in ministry. Then determine if you are together or separated. If separated, choose to change your ministry and worship focus so that you can be more together as a couple.

For it is written, "You shall worship the LORD your God, and him only you shall serve."

Luke 4:8

67 Find Ways to Give Generously to Each Other

Giving starts at home. I have met families that have actually deprived their children of food so they could give an offering.

Our primary responsibility is toward our marriage and families. We tithe and we sow extravagantly into our spouses and children, knowing that the kingdom harvest to come through them will see many people saved, healed and delivered.

Of course there is nothing wrong with sacrificing for the Lord's work. Giving up our stuff in order to give an offering must be part of our giving patterns. But we give generously at home to bless our family so they can fulfill their destiny in Christ.

How has your spouse experienced your extravagant generosity this week? How have you given freely of your time and money toward your spouse?

Try this: Save up and surprise your spouse with an extravagant gift that has no other motivation behind it than to say, "I love you extravagantly. This gift is the best of its kind that I can give you. I always want to give you my best."

Give, and it will be given to you: good measure,
pressed down, shaken together, and running over will
be put into your bosom. For with the same measure
that you use, it will be measured back to you.

Luke 6:38

68 TALK ABOUT JESUS

At times in the past, my wife would say, "You gave at the office. You have nothing left for me." And she was right. As a pastor, I would give all day long. When I arrived home I was completely drained.

I would talk about Jesus to everyone who would listen. But at home I talked about everything else—the kids, home repairs, the weather, church business, other people, etc.

Nothing's more exciting than talking about Jesus. Since He is the center of your marriage and family, He also needs to be the center of your conversation.

When was the last time you told your mate how much you loved Jesus or what He was doing in your life? Jesus said for us to be His witnesses first in Jerusalem and then in Judea, Samaria and to the uttermost parts of the earth. Jerusalem means "at home."

Try this: Watch a Jesus video. Talk about it with your spouse. Listen to the gospels on audio tape together. Talk about Jesus.

Sit down with your spouse for an hour and do nothing but share about what Jesus is doing in your life and marriage.

But you shall receive power when the Holy Spirit has come upon you; and you shall be witnesses to me in Jerusalem, and in all Judea and Samaria, and to the end of the earth.

Acts 1:8

69 Ask for Your Needs

No mate is omniscient. Ask for what you need. Some mates protest, "But after all these years of marriage he should know what I need." Not so.

Asking for our needs to be met can be the most important revelation of the moment in our marriages. At times we individually become so preoccupied with our own needs that we lose sight of what a mate may need. Don't bury your needs. Pray for those needs to be met. Ask your spouse to meet the realistic needs in your marriage.

Listed below are the top ten needs for marital intimacy identified by The Center for Marriage and Family Intimacy in Austin, Texas. Rank these needs according to your own personal priorities related to what you need in marriage:

_____ **Acceptance**. *Wherefore accept one another, just as Christ also accepted us to the glory of God.*

Rom. 15:7

_____ **Approval**. *Because anyone who serves Christ in this way is pleasing to God and approved by men.*

Rom. 14:18

_____ **Encouragement**. *Therefore encourage one another and build each other up . . .*

1 Thess. 5:11

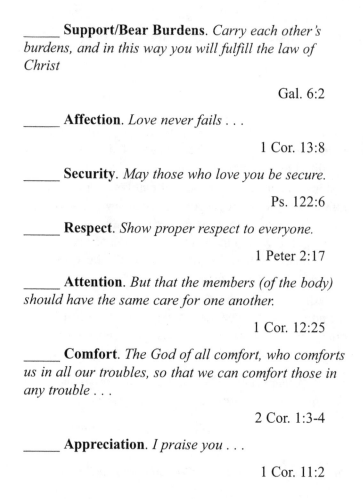

_____ **Support/Bear Burdens**. *Carry each other's burdens, and in this way you will fulfill the law of Christ*

Gal. 6:2

_____ **Affection**. *Love never fails . . .*

1 Cor. 13:8

_____ **Security**. *May those who love you be secure.*

Ps. 122:6

_____ **Respect**. *Show proper respect to everyone.*

1 Peter 2:17

_____ **Attention**. *But that the members (of the body) should have the same care for one another.*

1 Cor. 12:25

_____ **Comfort**. *The God of all comfort, who comforts us in all our troubles, so that we can comfort those in any trouble . . .*

2 Cor. 1:3-4

_____ **Appreciation**. *I praise you . . .*

1 Cor. 11:2

Try this: You and your spouse each rank these needs for yourself individually and then guess what the top three needs will be for your spouse. Share your lists with one another.

70 BE INTERDEPENDENT, NOT INDEPENDENT OR DEPENDENT

"I don't know what I will do if Bill dies," grieved the distraught wife at the bedside of her terminally ill husband. Dying of cancer in his 50s, his wife had become so dependant on him that she couldn't imagine living without him.

God calls us to become one in marriage, but He doesn't call us to lose our identity in our spouse. We are crucified with Christ, not to our mate's identity. One of Albert Ellis' irrational beliefs is, "I must depend on something or someone stronger than myself." Of course, we depend on God. But, we don't stake our existence on another person or thing.

Likewise, the opposite extreme of dependency can be dangerous. If we feel so independent from our spouse, then we live parallel but separate lives that lack intimacy and fulfillment of oneness or covenant in marriage. God's ideal of oneness is that we each have our own identity in Christ Jesus, but we also share an interdependence in our Christ-centered oneness. We need each other, not to live, but to serve Christ and each other with our best.

Try this: Share with your mate all the wonderful ways you need him or her. Or share all the awesome ways Christ's oneness shines through your marriage.

Two can accomplish more than twice as much as one,
for the results can be much better.
If one falls, the other pulls him up;
but if a man falls when he is alone, he is in trouble.

Eccl. 4:9-10 TLB

71 BE MORALLY ACCOUNTABLE
TO ONE ANOTHER

"**I** noticed that you looked lustfully at other women when we were at the beach," observed the wife.

"There's no harm in looking," replied the husband. A lengthy discussion followed that exchange, and a new depth of accountability began to develop between the husband and wife.

We honor our spouses with our eyes as well as with our hearts and minds. Let your eyes look straight ahead, counsels Proverbs 4:25. In other words, don't let your eyes lead you to look at evil. 1 John 2:16 reminds us, "For all that is in the world—the lust of the flesh, the lust of the eyes, and the pride of life—is not of the Father but is of the world."

Be morally accountable to your spouse as well as to another Christian, such as a mentor, small group member or same-gender friend who can speak truth into your life in love.

Have eyes only for your spouse. When you are out in public—at the beach, mall, or at work; and when you are on the computer, reading, or watching TV, movies, and videos. Share openly and honestly with one another about your physical and sexual needs. Guard your eyes and heart so that you do not dwell on unclean thoughts.

Try this: Make a checklist with your mate of those moral areas of your relationship where you will be accountable. Go over that list together weekly.

"You have heard that it was said,
'Do not commit adultery.' But I tell you
that anyone who looks at a woman lustfully
has already committed adultery with her in his heart."
Matt. 5:27-28 NIV

72 Share Financial Responsibility and Spending

"I have to pay all the bills," protested the wife. "He doesn't know and doesn't seem to care about what's happening. I am so stressed out!"

One partner cannot do all the money management and spending in a marriage. Who should keep the checkbook and pay the bills? While one spouse may do the bookkeeping, both are responsible for knowing all that's happening financially in a marriage.

It's hard to keep everything together financially in a marriage. Often, both spouses work just to make ends meet. Both may have stressful jobs that demand much time and energy.

Finances can become a major stress in marriage. But when the responsibility is shared, then both partners can feel that they are "in this together."

It's so helpful to sit down together and do the bills. It's insightful for both partners to go grocery shopping together. And it's fun to make a purchase together that both are agreed upon. So, are you willing to carry the financial load together? It's far easier when both mates are fully involved in managing and carrying family financial responsibilities.

Try this: Sit down and do the bills together. Talk about future financial goals and purchases. Be in agreement about finances. Go shopping together. Discuss finances when you are rested and not under great stress.

Can two walk together, unless they are agreed?

Amos 3:3

73 NEVER OWN ANYTHING

In his booklet, *Five Spiritual Laws*, A.W. Tozer writes that we should never own anything. Anything we possess ultimately possesses us. The focus in our lives is not on possessing, but rather on stewardship.

We may be stewards of a number of things in our lives; all that we have belongs to Jesus. We do not even own our bodies in marriage. We willingly give ourselves to one another. Let the husband render to his wife the affection due her, and likewise also the wife to her husband. The wife does not have authority over her own body, but the husband does. And likewise the husband does not have authority over his own body, but the wife does (1 Cor. 7:3-4).

Holding on tightly to stuff will cause marital conflict. Why? Because the stuff can become more important to us than each other. Money, homes, cars, and material possessions are simply tools to be used to serve our families, others, and God. I heard a truism a number of years ago that has much wisdom: "We use stuff and love people; we do not use people and love stuff." What about your stuff? Are you living for it or living for Christ?

Try this: Spend time together discussing everything that you have. Ask, "Do we really need this?" "How does this serve our family, others and the Lord?" "What lasting purpose does this thing have in God's plans for our lives?"

"For everyone to whom much is given, from him much will be required; and to whom much has been committed, of him they will ask the more."

Luke 12:48

74 SET RIGHT PRIORITIES: GOD FIRST, MARRIAGE AND FAMILY AND THEN THE REST

Too many spouses put work or even church ahead of their families and marriages. Their work or church activities actually rob valuable time and intimacy from the family.

First maintain your relationship with God through worship, Bible study, prayer, spiritual disciplines, giving, witnessing and serving the Lord. You can share much together spiritually as a couple. Pray, worship, serve God and read Scripture together.

Next make your marriage and family your first priority in life. True, you may spend many hours at work. But when you are together, give one another your full attention and devotion. You work to live; you don't live to work. Give quality time to your spouse and your family.

As a wise mentor in ministry once asked me, "How is your mistress?" I was shocked and replied indignantly that I didn't have a mistress. "Oh, I mean your work at church," he replied. True enough, I was so enamored with my work that I treated my church like a mistress. Much had to change … and it did!

Try this: Make a weekly calendar together. Write down when you will spend time together. Look forward to your moments of sharing, praying and simply being together. Make your spouse the neighbor you love first!

> *"And you shall love the LORD your God with all your heart, with all your soul, with all your mind, and with all your strength." This is the first commandment. And the second, like it, is this: 'You shall love your neighbor as yourself.'*

Matt. 12:30-31

81

75 SHARE TRANSPARENTLY TO ELIMINATE THE NEED FOR EXCUSES

"I never know what you really mean," protested a frustrated spouse. Vague reassurances never pay the bills. Confusing excuses never make up for deep hurts. It's time to come clean with one another in your marriage.

So how do you become transparent when it's so risky? If we are too open, then another person has all "the goods" on us. They know our secrets and our deepest needs. They can hurt or betray us at any time. That's the risk of being transparent.

But the benefits of transparency far outweigh the risks. When we are open and speak the truth in love, then we grow deeper in our love and intimacy with one another. Some people use openness as an excuse for cruelty. This isn't what we mean.

Openness allows for an intimacy that says, "Into me see." See my strengths and my weaknesses. See my dreams and my nightmares. See my hope and my despair. Know me. Help me carry this burden to Christ.

Besides God, our mate is the person with whom we can become truly transparent. Without transparency, we miss the close friendship that every marriage needs. Partners work together, but mates are more than partners. In marriage we are one in Christ.

Try this: Spend time weekly sharing your goals, aspirations, dreams, hopes, and also your failures, sins, mistakes and feelings of inadequacy. Encourage one another.

Bear one another's burdens, and so fulfill the law of Christ.

Gal. 6:2

76 Get Out of Debt; Get the Debt Out of You

"We'll never get all these credit cards paid off," moaned a distressed spouse. Yes, you can and must. Some financial counselors advise no debt whatsoever, including mortgages. But it's impossible to get to that utopia without first destroying credit card debt.

Decide to cut up your cards and close the accounts. Begin to live within your income, not outside of it. What's more important is to get the debt out of you. Stop impulse buying. Refuse the temptation to get what you want when you want it. Instead, plan your purchases and save for them.

Getting the debt out of you also involves releasing a victim- or poverty-mentality. You are not poor. You have a rich God who blesses you with abundance both materially and spiritually. But you will never break free of a poverty-mentality until you see yourself rich in Christ Jesus. Getting the debt out of you can begin with becoming a giver. Decide to tithe and give offerings. Become a giver instead of a hoarder. Without sowing, you will never have a future harvest that will prosper both you and your children.

Try this: Choose a credit card to pay off and do it as soon as possible. Cut it up and close the account. Take the money your were paying on that card and apply it to the next. Pay if off. Keep the cycle going until you get out of debt. Start tithing and giving to God. Become a cheerful giver.

So let each one give as he purposes in his heart, not grudgingly or of necessity; for God loves a cheerful giver cheerful giver

2 Cor. 9:7

77 ENCOURAGE ONE ANOTHER

Some mates believe they have certain rights and entitlements in marriage. The best place to dump your imagined rights isn't on your spouse; it's at the foot of the cross. Try this: If we have any indisputable rights in marriage, they are as follows. Say to your mate:

THE MARRIAGE BILL OF RIGHTS

I have the right to encourage you daily.

I have the right to build you up, not tear you down.

I have the right to affirm you every time you succeed.

I have the right to encourage you every time you win or lose.

I have the right to comfort you when you hurt.

I have the right to protect you when you are attacked.

I have right to pray for you without ceasing.

I have the right to defend you from every weapon formed against you.

I have the right to esteem and honor you.

I have the right to pick you up when you fall.

I have the right to speak life to you.

I have the right to love you unconditionally.

I have the right to respect you in front of others.

I have the right to find out your needs and meet them, and to diagnose your hurts and heal them.

I have the right to serve you at any time.

I have the right to ask God to give you wisdom.
I have the right to bless you.

So encourage each other to build each other up, just as you are already doing.

1 Thess. 5:11 TLB

POSTSCRIPT

These truths have not been placed in any strategic or significant order. You and your spouse will need to prioritize them according to where your marriage relationship is right now.

We simply want to leave you with this thought. Marriage is for life. Marriage is a covenant so important to God that He created it first and likened His relationship with us to marriage.

Read the Song of Songs together. Enjoy the beautiful intimacy that the Word imparts to marriage. Pass this book on to your children and friends. Find ways to strengthen your marriage. Most of all, pray. Remember that prayer is the language of spiritual intimacy in marriage.

Father God, thank you for the spouses reading this book. Bring blessing, wholeness, restoration and healing to every marriage. In Jesus' name, Amen.

OTHER BOOKS BY DR. LARRY KEEFAUVER

Lord, I Wish My Husband Would Pray with Me
Lord, I Wish My Teenager Would Talk with Me
Lord, I Wish My Family Would Get Saved
Hugs for Grandparents
When God Doesn't Heal Now
Experiencing the Holy Spirit
Praying with Smith Wigglesworth
Smith Wigglesworth on Prayer
Smith Wigglesworth on Faith
Smith Wigglesworth on Healing
Healing Words
I'm Praying for You, Friend
I'm Praying for You, Mom
The Holy Spirit Encounter Guides
    (Anointing,
    Welcoming the Spirit, Gifts, Power,
    The Spirit-Led Life, River, Fire)
Prayers of the Presidents

DR. LARRY & JUDI KEEFAUVER

The 77 Irrefutable Truths of Parenting
The 77 Irrefutable Truths of Ministry
The 77 Irrefutable Truths of Prayer

CONFERENCES AND SEMINARS

Growing Spiritually in Marriage
Proactive Parenting Seminars
77 Irrefutable Truths of Ministry
A Holy Spirit Encounter
The Presence-Driven Life, Family and Church
Inviting God's Presence

FOR INFORMATION OR TO ORDER BOOKS CONTACT:

Dr. Larry Keefauver
Your Ministry Counseling Services
P.O. Box 950596
Lake Mary, Fl 32795

800-750-5306 (Voice)
Email: lkeefauv@bellsouth.net or larry@ymcs.org
Website: www.ymcs.org

If you were encouraged by **77 Irrefutable Truths of Marriage** you will want to read the Keefauvers next book in the series, **77 Irrefutable Truths of Prayer**

Dr. Larry & Judi Keefauver

Seventy Seven Irrefutable Truths of Prayer

ISBN 0-88270-9097
Available at fine Christian bookstores worldwide